HORSES

BY CYNTHIA AMOROSO AND BOB NOYED

PUBLISHED BY THE CHILD'S WORLD®

The Child's World®
childsworld.com

Published by The Child's World®
1980 Lookout Drive • Mankato, MN 56003-1705
800-599-READ • www.childsworld.com

ACKNOWLEDGMENTS
The Child's World®: Mary Swensen, Publishing Director
The Design Lab: Design
Michael Miller: Editing
Sarah M. Miller: Editing

DESIGN ELEMENTS
© Doremi/Shutterstock.com

PHOTO CREDITS
© acceptphoto/Shutterstock.com: cover; eastern light photography/
Shutterstock.com: 6; Gregory Johnston/Shutterstock.com: 19;
Gualberto Becerra/Shutterstock.com: 11; Irina Mos/Shutterstock.
com: 16-17; mariait/Shutterstock.com: 10; Nate Allred/Shutterstock.
com: 15; Olga_i/Shutterstock.com: 8-9; Rita Kochmarjova/
Shutterstock.com: 20-21; Tomas K/Shutterstock.com: 12; Vera
Zinkova/Shutterstock.com: 5

ISBN: 9781503808287
LCCN: 2015958481

Printed in the United States of America
Mankato, MN
June, 2016
PA02308

Table of Contents

Cute Horses

Horses are large animals with four strong legs. They have **hooves** on their feet. Horses make a "na-a-a-y" sound.

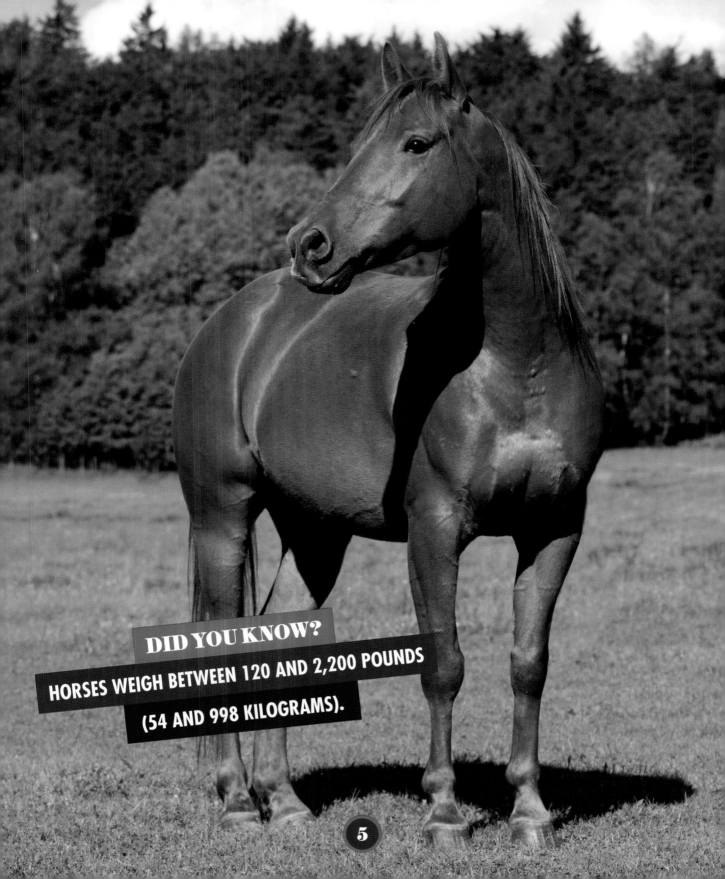

DID YOU KNOW?

HORSES WEIGH BETWEEN 120 AND 2,200 POUNDS (54 AND 998 KILOGRAMS).

DID YOU KNOW?

HORSES CAN SLEEP LYING DOWN

OR STANDING UP.

Long Bodies

Horses have long necks and long noses. They have long hair down their necks. This hair is called a **mane**.

Horses have long tails, too. Their tails swing back and forth all day.

DID YOU KNOW?

HORSES RUN ABOUT 40 MILES PER HOUR (64 KILOMETERS PER HOUR).

Males and Females

Some male horses are called **stallions**. Other male horses are called **geldings**.

Female horses are called **mares**. Mares are calmer than stallions.

Foals

A baby horse is called
a **foal**. Foals like to run
and play. They drink their
mother's milk. Then they
learn to nibble grass.

Eating

Horses eat many things.
They eat oats, **barley**, and
corn. Horses love to eat
grass, too.

DID YOU KNOW?
HORSES LIKE TO EAT APPLES AND CARROTS FOR TREATS.

15

DID YOU KNOW?

HORSES CAN TURN THEIR EARS ALMOST ALL THE WAY AROUND.

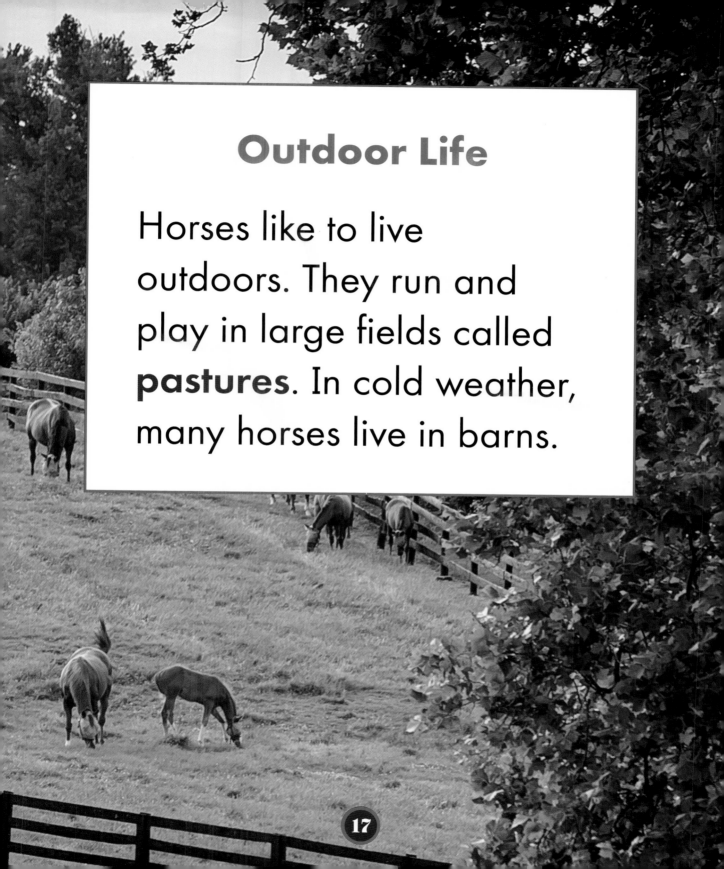

Outdoor Life

Horses like to live outdoors. They run and play in large fields called **pastures**. In cold weather, many horses live in barns.

Important Horses

Horses are smart and friendly animals. They are strong and can pull wagons and carts. Horses have been used for work for hundreds of years.

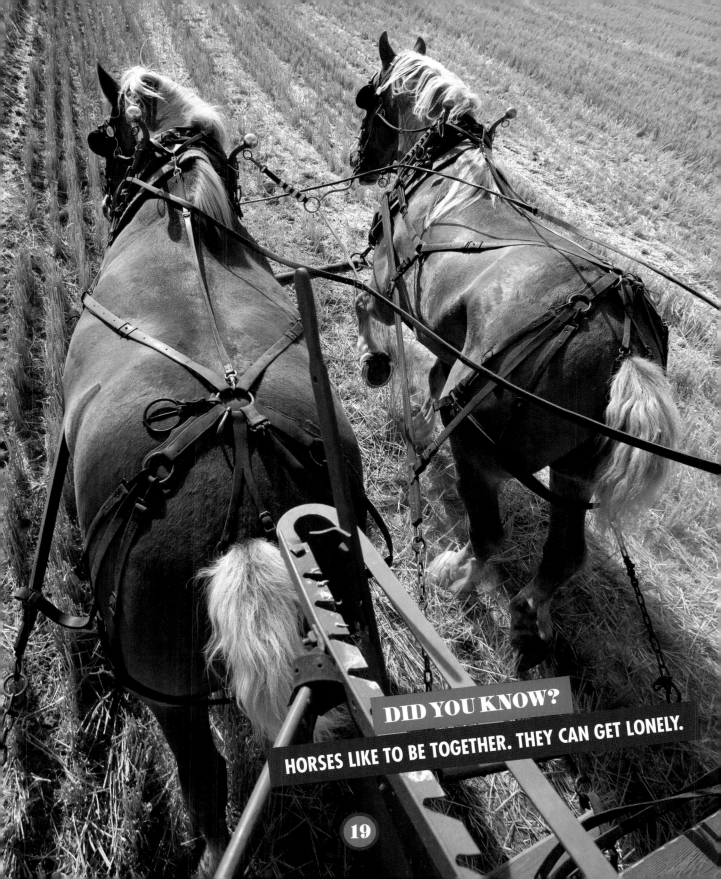

DID YOU KNOW?

HORSES LIKE TO BE TOGETHER. THEY CAN GET LONELY.

DID YOU KNOW?

HORSES SLEEP ONLY ABOUT FOUR HOURS PER DAY.

Many horses live just as pets. They are fun to ride and make good friends for people.

Glossary

BARLEY (BAR-lee) Barley is a kind of grain that farm horses like to eat.

FOAL (FOHL) A foal is a baby horse.

GELDINGS (GEL-dingz) Geldings are male horses that cannot mate with females.

HOOVES (HOOVZ) Hooves are hard coverings that some animals have on their feet.

MANE (MAYN) The hair on a horse's neck is its mane.

MARES (MAYRZ) Mares are female horses.

PASTURES (PASS-churz) Pastures are large areas of grassy land where animals can rest, play, and eat.

STALLIONS (STAL-yunz) Stallions are male horses.

To Learn More

IN THE LIBRARY

Blazeman, Christopher. *Horses Up Close*. Huntington Beach, CA: Teacher Created Materials, 2012.

Crisp, Marty. *Everything Horse: What Kids Really Want to Know about Horses*. Minnetonka, MN: NorthWord, 2005.

Simon, Seymour. *Horses*. New York, NY: HarperCollins Publishers, 2006.

ON THE WEB

Visit our Web site for links about horses:
childsworld.com/links

Note to Parents, Teachers, and Librarians: We routinely verify our Web links to make sure they are safe and active sites. So encourage your readers to check them out!

Index

ABOUT THE AUTHORS

Cynthia Amoroso is an assistant superintendent in a Minnesota school district. She enjoys reading, writing, gardening, traveling, and spending time with friends and family.

Bob Noyed has worked in school communications and public relations. He continues to write for both children and adult audiences. Bob lives in Woodbury, Minnesota.